amodernmix

machine & hand quilting

Anita Shackelford

American Quilter's Society

P. O. Box 3290 • Paducah, KY 42002-3290

www.AmericanQuilter.com

Located in Paducah, Kentucky, the American Quilter's Society (AQS) is dedicated to promoting the accomplishments of today's quilters. Through its publications and events, AQS strives to honor today's quiltmakers and their work and to inspire future creativity and innovation in quiltmaking.

EDITOR: BONNIE K. BROWNING
GRAPHIC DESIGN: ELAINE WILSON
COVER DESIGN: MICHAEL BUCKINGHAM
PHOTOGRAPHY: CHARLES R. LYNCH
HOW-TO PHOTOGRAPHY: ANITA SHACKELFORD

Library of Congress Cataloging-in-Publication Data

Shackelford, Anita.

    A modern mix: machine and hand quilting / by Anita Shackelford.

       p. cm.

    Summary: "Learn how to successfully incorporate hand and machine quilting in the same quilt. Guidelines for planning your quilt, including thread and design selection. Provides several quilting designs and methods including backgrounds, borders, and more. Quilting projects complete with patterns, instructions, and full-size quilting patterns included"--Provided by publisher.

    Includes bibliographical references.

    ISBN 978-1-57432-938-4

    1. Machine Quilting. 2. Patchwork. 3. Quilting. I. Title.

    TT835.S4625 2007

    746.46'041--dc22

          2007032676

Additional copies of this book may be ordered from the American Quilter's Society, PO Box 3290, Paducah, KY 42002-3290, or online at www.AmericanQuilter.com. For phone orders only 800-626-5420. For all other inquiries, call 270-898-7903.

Proudly printed and bound in the United States of America

LEFT AND OPPOSITE: **POINSETTIA**, details, made by the author.

acknowledgments

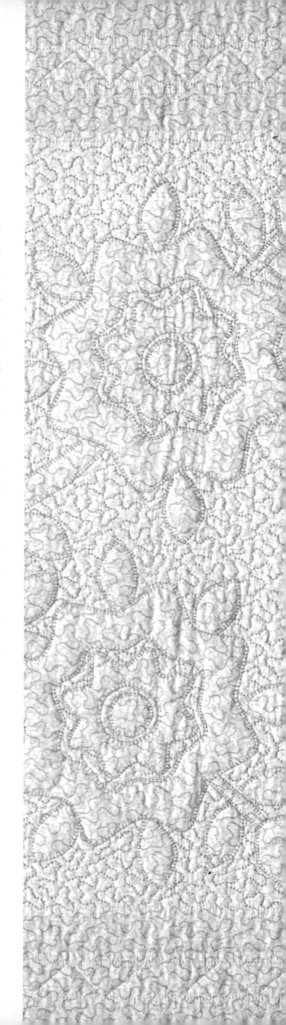

When I started quilting in the 1960s, almost every quilt was traditional in style and made by hand. Things have changed dramatically as quilting has come into its modern age. I've made changes along the way, too and have discovered how easily hand and machine techniques can be combined. Adding machine quilting to my list of skills has also brought me into a whole new circle of friends. I'm not leaving the old, just widening the circle and enriching the experience. As with all the other books I have written, many people have supported my efforts and made contributions along the way. To them I am grateful.

To my family, especially my husband, Richard, who has shared this journey from the beginning and always gives me the time I need to be creative.

To my daughter, Jennifer Shackelford Perdue, who is beginning to travel this road with me and will surely make her own mark in the quilting world.

To Bill and Meredith Schroeder for their unfailing support of the art of quilting, and to the staff at AQS who have made important contributions to this book – Bonnie Browning, Charles Lynch, Elaine Wilson, and Michael Buckingham.

To the friends who have shared their quilts and special talents to be included here – Janice Bahrt, Todd Brown, Martha Creasy, Kim Diamond, Tammy Finkler, Diane Gaudynski, Rene Jennings, Linda McCuean, Jennifer Perdue, Andi Perejda, Paul Statler, Sharon Stroud, and Linda Taylor. Thank you all.

To my students who continue to enjoy my work and to everyone who loves quilting in any form.

Keep the tradition alive.

Contents

OPPOSITE: EASY, BREEZY LEAVES. Made by the author.

introduction

I remember waking up early in the morning to the sound of my grandmother's wringer washing machine. It had a pounding rhythm, a churning, swishing sound that told me what she was doing. I would find her standing by the washer, watching it work. She fed the clothes, by hand, through the wringer into the rinse water, then again through the wringer, before putting them into the basket and hanging them to dry. Grandma also made her quilts by hand.

My mother's generation was thrilled with the technological advances that gave them the automatic washing machine. No more hand work! She could even walk away from the machine and do something else. What a time saver. Today, we take an automatic washing machine for granted, but still there are those few things I like to wash by hand.

Next came the clothes dryer and although my mother had one for a long time, she still preferred to hang her clothes outside to dry. It was nice to have the choice depending on the particular garment, the weather, or her energy that day.

My generation has had the choice of washing dishes by hand or using a dishwasher. I was slower to accept this machine, thinking that it was too much of a luxury. But I still remember the first evening that I used it. I was sitting on the front porch, when a neighbor went by and asked what I was doing. "Washing the dishes!" was my quick reply. I still wash a number of things by hand – fragile items, good knives, large sticky pots – but the majority of the work is done by machine.

I've been quilting by hand since the late 1960s. I love hand quilting; it's a calm and relaxing process, and I have finished nearly 200 pieces this way. I've been using a sewing machine since I was a teenager, making clothing and home decorator items, but I didn't use it on my quilts. The purchase of a new sewing machine

LEFT: FRIENDSHIP LILIES, detail. Designed by the author. Machine quilting by Diane Gaudynski. Hand quilting and Sashiko by the author.

in the mid-1980s gave me the option of quilting with a walking foot. I started experimenting with quilting in the ditch and simple line patterns in borders. I discovered (as many already knew) that it was a quicker way to finish a few things. Although I never took the time to learn free-motion quilting, I found that simple flowing designs could be stitched with the walking foot. Some areas were quicker and easier to quilt by machine and some were still easier by hand. It made sense to use the technique that fit the situation and gave me a good finished product.

Our new generation is fortunate to have many different ways to quilt. Together, my daughter, Jennifer, and I have been quilting with a longarm machine. We are not choosing one technique over the other because one is better than the other. The decision is not about which method is right or better or faster or easier, but how to achieve the effect we want. By combining hand and machine quilting in the same piece, we can have the best of both worlds.

We can use hand piecing, machine piecing, hand appliqué, machine appliqué, hand quilting, or machine quilting. Most quilters have a favorite way of working. We like to piece by machine, now that we have new methods to make it easy and accurate. Hand piecing has also found a new audience, but often those hand-pieced blocks are set together by machine. And many of us wouldn't hesitate to combine machine piecing with hand appliqué. We should choose the techniques that make us comfortable with the work and give us the best results. A mix of quilting techniques can serve us in the same way. There are many ways and many good reasons to combine hand and machine quilting in the same quilt. In the project section you will find bed quilts, wall quilts, and other small pieces, along with notes about how each was quilted. Make the projects shown or study the notes for inspiration in your own work.

From a practical point of view, hand quilters might ask themselves, "How many quilts can a hand quilter finish in a lifetime?" Working with a combination of hand and machine quilting can help us make more quilts. We can "save" our hands by putting only measured amounts of handwork into each quilt.

Most of us make quilts for our family to use or to keep. I have made both kinds of quilts for my children and grandchildren. I want them to grow up knowing and loving quilts. The heirloom quilts are hand quilted, but I would never think of putting that much time into a quilt for them to use everyday. It makes sense to make sturdy machine-quilted quilts for children to use. But, at the same time, think about including some hand quilting for them to see. Most of us feel a strong sense of connection to the handwork of a previous generation and we can touch future generations in the same way. As a variation on this idea, think about machine quilting the quilt and hand quilting a pillow or two to go with it. Or, hand quilt the front of a pillow and machine quilt the back.

Perhaps working with a friend will be the reason you choose to put hand and machine quilting into the same quilt. Working with a partner can be fun. If you each have different quilting skills, why not combine them? Think about ways to combine hand quilting and sewing machine, hand quilting and longarm, or sewing machine and longarm quilting.

Once you begin to think about reasons to combine quilting techniques, chances are you will find many more combinations and good ways to use them.

planning the quilt:
a good mix

Whan you visualize an overall plan for quilting, assess the mood of the quilt and think about what style of quilting will best complement the design of the top.

Start with questions like these:
- ✻ Does the design need to be quilted a piece at a time, with traditional lines following the patchwork and in the ditch, and with separate motifs filling the open spaces?
- ✻ Should lines run across the top in a flowing or abstract way?
- ✻ Can quilting lines be used to add contour or texture to the design?
- ✻ Will it be necessary to quilt through many layers, fused appliqué, or many seam lines?
- ✻ Does the design need traditional quilting lines to fill the space behind appliqué?
- ✻ What will be the best choice for the borders?
- ✻ Where will hand quilting be most effective?

Consider how the quilt will be used.
- ✻ Is it an heirloom for the family to keep?
- ✻ A show quilt which must stand up to close inspection?
- ✻ A quilt to be displayed on a bed?
- ✻ One to be used by a child?
- ✻ Art to hang on the wall?

All of these questions will help evaluate what part of the quilting should be done by hand and what part by machine. Some are technical answers while some are based on design.

LEFT AND OPPOSITE: BLOSSOMING IN A NEW CENTURY. Long seam lines are machine quilted with a walking foot; background grid in the blocks is quilted by hand.

A good way to begin might be to machine quilt in the ditch, with a sewing machine and walking foot, or longarm machine, along the main joining seams or block construction lines. Quilting in the ditch is usually hidden by the fold of the seam. Ditch quilting is not the most effective place to use hand quilting time and talent. Seams are less flexible, making this area more difficult to quilt by hand. Long seams may be easier to do with the sewing machine and a walking foot. Be sure the weight of the quilt is supported as it moves through the machine so that it doesn't drag or pull the quilt out of position. Use a little tension on both sides of the seam, to pull the ditch open, but not so much as to pull the seam out of alignment. It should be a simple matter to lay an almost invisible line of machine quilting in any seam line.

Long lines of machine quilting across a quilt add stability and structure, making it more stable to move in and out of a hoop for areas of hand quilting.

LEFT: **FEATHERED STAR.** Floral **motifs show well in the background spaces of this wall quilt. See the pattern on page 87.**

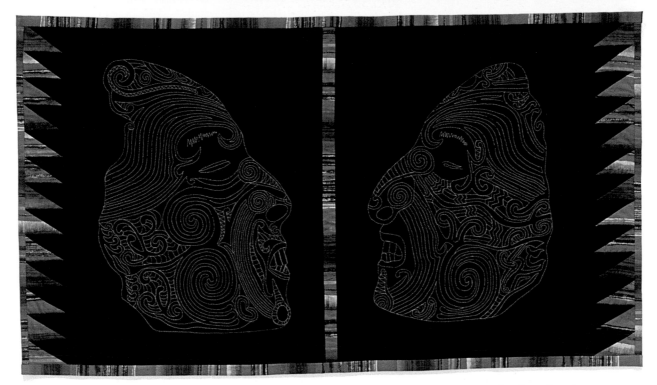

ABOVE: **WARRIORS, made by Andi Perejda. Complex line drawings were stitched by machine and then the background was hand quilted.**

BELOW: **Fancy quilting shows best on plain fabric.**

Fancy designs are perfect for open areas on a quilt. This is the place they will show best. Feathers, flowers, and other realistic images can be quilted with a longarm machine, a sewing machine, or by hand, depending on one's skills.

An interesting combination might be to quilt fancy, continuous-line designs by machine and then add the start-and-stop background lines by hand.

Or, reversing that idea, hand quilt the detail quilting first, and then add machine stipple quilting to the background.

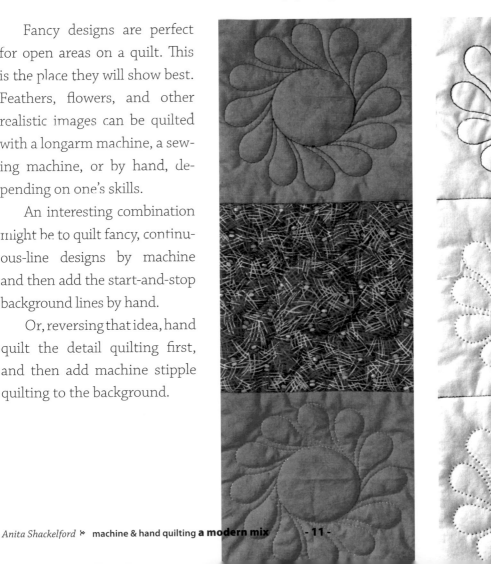

Because a machine-quilted line is visually stronger than a hand quilted line, consider using darker thread for the hand quilting and a matching color or invisible thread for the machine stippling.

With a combination of quilting techniques, you can reserve hand quilting for solid fabrics or background areas where it will show to its best advantage. Use machine quilting in the areas where the hand quilting would not show, such as busy prints. Because machine quilting is a continuous line of stitches, it is more likely to stand out on patterned fabric.

Long, curvilinear lines should flow smoothly across the surface of the quilt. Better control might be achieved when designs, such as cables, are quilted with a walking foot or by hand rather than free-motion machine quilting.

Quilting in the ditch around appliqué emphasizes the motif by raising it up from the surface of the quilt. Most appliqué shapes are complex, with many changes of direction. The quilting line should surround the appliqué, exactly against the edge or a small, measured distance away. The stitching should not run up over the edge, as can sometimes happen with free-motion machine quilting. Quilting around an appliqué shape is probably most accurate when done by hand.

LEFT: **Complex cable – back side of HUNTER'S SQUARE**

RIGHT: **PARADISE POPPY. Hand quilting is an accurate way to outline appliqué shapes. Custom-dyed batik fabrics from SewBatik™.**

Echo quilting can be measured and marked for hand or machine quilting. Use your favorite marking pencil and a compass to draw lines an even distance from the edge of a shape, repeating over and over until the background space is filled. Echo quilting can also be measured with a walking foot or hopping foot when machine quilting.

Quilting background lines behind dimensional work will also be easiest by hand. Lift the edges of the appliqué and extend the line of quilting so that it disappears behind the dimensional piece.

Consider the ease of quilting in each area of the quilt. A sewing machine or longarm machine will easily quilt through many layers of fabric, such as areas of complex piecing, layered appliqué, or fused layers. Save hand quilting for the softer parts.

Blocks, sashing strips, and borders can be framed and finished with a line of stitching ¼" away from the seam lines. Use the edge of the walking foot to measure the placement so the lines of stitching run parallel to each other.

Echo quilting lines can be measured with a walking foot.

Echo quilting can be done using a free-motion foot.

LEFT: Echo quilting by hand around appliqué on TROPICAL BREEZES

Quilting close to dimensional work – SPRING BOUQUET with ruched flowers

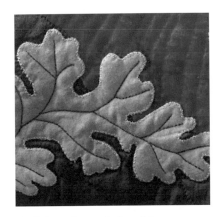

Quilting through fused layers on the POPPY pillow

A walking foot can be used along a border seam so the lines run parallel.

RIGHT: EASY, BREEZY LEAVES, detail. Quilting across seam lines will be easier by machine.

Borders can sometimes be half of the quilt surface and usually take a great deal of time to quilt. Machine quilting the borders is one of the simplest and most timesaving of choices. It is also less physically demanding than machine quilting the center, because when you quilt a border, the bulk of the quilt is out from under the sewing machine. Hand quilting the center of the quilt and machine quilting the borders is a great combination.

LEFT: **COXCOMB ALBUM**, detail. Outline and detail quilting of appliqué and background patterns are quilted by hand. In-the-ditch, sashing, and border-grid patterns are quilted by machine.

RIGHT: **COXCOMB ALBUM**, detail

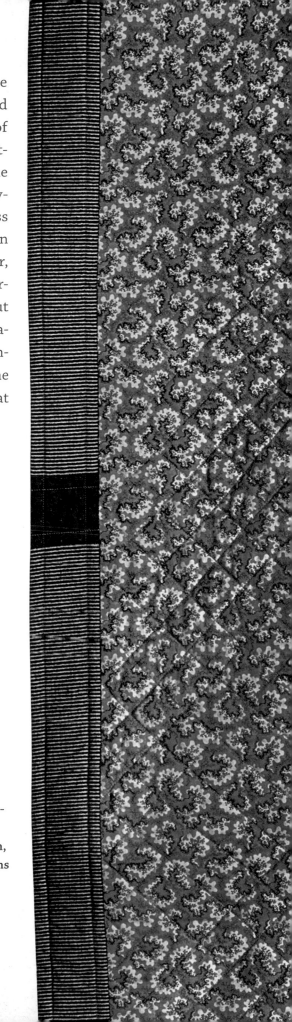

Some sewing machines and longarm machines can be controlled by a computer to quilt a perfect pattern in almost any space. After the patterned quilting is finished, additional quilting can be added by hand or sewing machine. Perhaps the quilt will need a line of stitching in the ditch to separate the center from the border, a few lines of hand quilting in the background, or detail lines on appliquéd pieces, such a veins on leaves or lines on petals.

LEFT: **Computer-controlled pattern – BABY BASKET. Border patterns and Pumpkinseed from Precision Stitch/Statler Stitcher; feather designs by the author. Ditch quilting is done by sewing machine using a walking foot. Background quilting is stitched by hand.**

ABOVE: **Programmed stitches (Bernina) add a serpentine pattern to the border of ARIZONA SUNFLOWER. Ditch quilting is done by sewing machine using a walking foot. Background quilting is stitched by hand.**

Longarm free-motion or computer-controlled designs are a beautiful choice to fill open blocks or to quilt a pattern over patchwork. Quilting which is isolated within the blocks usually leaves the quilt looking incomplete. Adding a line of quilting in the ditch to define and frame blocks and borders will add a finished look to the quilt. Use the longarm to quilt in the ditch, or use the sewing machine and a walking foot to add quilting in all of the long seams.

ABOVE: **OHIO BICENTENNIAL. The quilt shows before and after quilting along the long seams.**

Be sure the quilting design fits the mood of the quilt. Choose a design in the same style or one that repeats the theme of the fabrics used in the quilt. Sharon Stroud pieced a sampler quilt using a black background and a variety of chili-pepper colors. The allover chili-pepper quilting design adds to the theme of the quilt and the variegated thread shows well on the black fabric.

LEFT AND OPPOSITE: **SALSA. Pieced by Sharon Stroud, quilted by the author. Quilting pattern designed and digitized by Kim Diamond.**

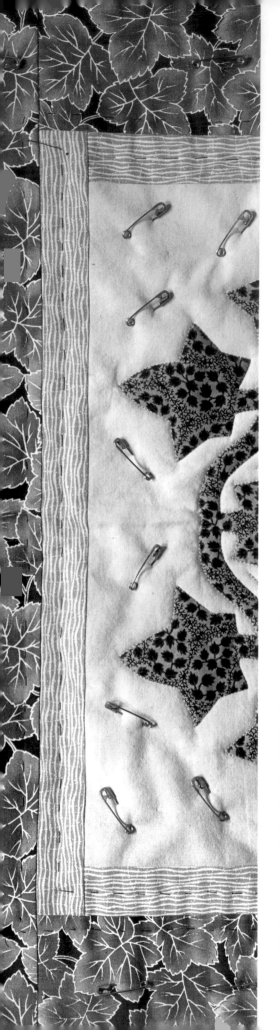

preparing the quilt top

Think about the quilting process as the top is being made. When quilters use a walking foot to quilt in the ditch, most have a preference for quilting on the right side or the left side of the seam line. This is more visual than mechanical, but it does seem to make a difference in the ease and accuracy of the quilting. Because in-the-ditch quilting should always be done on the "low" side, the side without the seam allowance, you can prepare your quilt top to suit your quilting preference. Press long seams toward the center of the quilt if quilting on the right side of the seam is easier for you; press seams toward the outside of the quilt if quilting on the left side of the seam is easier.

If you are planning large amounts of free-motion quilting which run across seam lines, a better plan might be to press some smaller seams open. This will make it easier for the walking foot or hopping foot (on a longarm machine) to travel across the surface and not be caught by a bulky intersection.

Layering and Basting the Quilt

Layering the quilt carefully will help ensure the piece finishes straight and square, with a smooth surface, front and back. To begin, spread the layers of the quilt on a carpeted floor. Pin the quilt lining to the carpet, using even tension throughout. A little tension on the lining will help prevent wrinkles, which otherwise could be quilted into the back of the quilt. Layer the batting and the quilt top individually, smoothing each as you go. Use a long T-square on the quilt top to check that long seam lines, sashings, etc. are straight

LEFT AND OPPOSITE: **IVY WREATH quilt layered and basted. Thread basting keeps sashings, borders, and other long seams straight.**

and true. Cross seams should run perpendicular to long seams and corners should be square. When the quilt is straight and square, use long straight pins to pin the layers together at the corners and along the sides. Thread basting will be most effective for keeping the long seam lines straight. Baste along the center of each sashing strip. Baste each border seam, parallel to, but not in, the ditch. Use small basting stitches for better control of the layers.

Once you have secured the major structure lines, use safety pins or tacks to secure all other areas. Many quilters think thread basting is only for hand quilting and that they should use safety pins or tacks for machine quilting. A combination of thread basting and safety pins gives good results. Long lines that have been thread basted are less likely to shift. By using fewer pins, the quilt will be lighter and easier to handle whether quilting by hand or machine. Fewer pins will also make it less likely to catch on the machine foot.

Quilts which are loaded onto the longarm frame do not require basting. The layers of the quilt are attached to the rollers, with each layer being smoothed and straightened individually. The longarm machine can also serve as a useful tool for those who want to quilt by hand or with their sewing machine. Layers can be placed on the frame and basted together with washout thread or regular thread. The quilt can then be removed for quilting.

ABOVE: IVY WREATH, detail. Finer basting stitches control raw edges.

It is important to baste the outside edges of the quilt to keep the layers together and to keep the edges from stretching or shifting while it is being quilted and as the binding is applied. Use a running stitch by hand and make stitches $\frac{1}{4}$" to $\frac{1}{2}$" apart to hold the raw edges of the quilt top in place. Another advantage to basted edges is that basting stitches can be pulled slightly to "correct" the length of the edge, if needed, before the binding is applied.

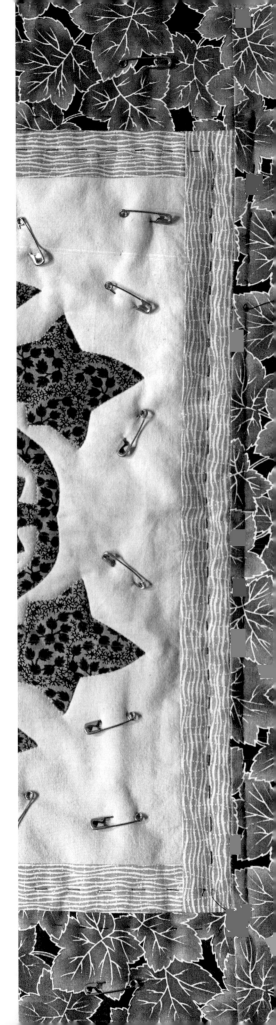

background patterns

Open background areas of a quilt can be filled with a variety of designs. The spacing and flow of the lines will affect both the visual texture and the softness of the piece. Technically, backgrounds are quilted to help stabilize the layers and control the fullness of the fabric and batting. From a design standpoint, background patterns make other elements, such as appliqué or large-scaled quilting motifs, more prominent.

Depending on the design chosen, background patterns can simply fill the space or they can add visual interest to the design. Ideally, there should be some contrast of line behind the motif, either in spacing, style, or direction. Fine quilting will help emphasize motifs in the foreground. Too much quilting can make a piece feel stiff. A good rule of thumb is to make the spacing of the background lines smaller than the smallest motif you hope to showcase. Appliqué with flowing lines may benefit from the contrast of straight line or grid quilting, while geometric patchwork can be softened with curved quilting lines. Diagonal background lines offer a pleasing contrast to strong vertical or horizontal elements.

Echo

An echo quilting pattern follows the shape of appliqué, and then repeats around itself until the background has been filled. Echoing is an effective way to emphasize a motif or

The echo-quilting design is evenly spaced around a flower shape.

LEFT AND OPPOSITE: **ENGLISH POPPY**, hand appliquéd, hand and machine quilted by the author. Straight background lines are a pleasing contrast to the appliqué.

to add movement to a design. On a large, traditional Hawaiian quilt, quilting lines might be placed ½" to ⅜" apart. Lines ¼" apart will be in better proportion for smaller, finer appliqué motifs. If you are marking the background for hand quilting, place a fabric marking pencil in a compass and use it to echo the shape until the background space is filled. Machine quilters often use the width of the presser foot or hopping foot to measure the spacing. The interior of the appliqué can also be echo quilted or details can be added to complement the mood of the design.

Echo quilting can be done with a walking foot

Echo quilting can be done on a longarm using the hopping foot to measure the distance.

Grid

A grid background design will be most accurate if the spacing is measured and marked along the sides of a block, rather than by measuring the spacing from one line to another. Follow these directions to draw a perfect background grid.

1. Measure the edge(s) of the block.

2. Find a number that divides evenly into that measurement.
    An even measurement, such as 12" or 18", can be divided every two inches. Odd sizes such as 9" or 7½" can be divided by 1½".
    For a block with an irregular size, such as 17", try dividing by the closest logical measurement, such as 2", which would yield a repeat of about 8 times. The final calculation would be 17" divided by 8 = 2.125; the spacing will be 2⅛" apart.

3. Mark the desired spacing along each side of the block.

4. Draw a line from corner to corner. Add diagonal lines, parallel to the first line, by drawing from dot to dot.

5. Do the same in the other direction to create a uniform grid.

This method ensures that the grid pattern fits the block, fills the space, and comes out even at the edges or seam lines.

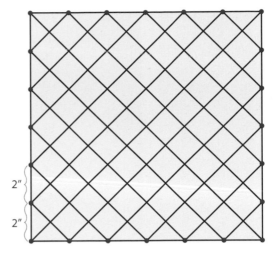

2"

2"

Basic grid lines measured and marked

Instead of marking every side of every block in a large quilt, mark the pattern on four pieces of masking tape. Use the tape to frame the block; mark or quilt the lines and then move the tape to the next block. The tape method also works well for irregular spacing, ensuring accuracy and saving the time of finding an unusual measurement over and over. And the best part is, with tape, there are no marks on the edges of the block.

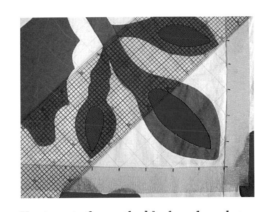

Use tape to frame the block and mark or quilt the lines.

Diamond Grid

For rectangular blocks, use the same number of divisions along each side, regardless of the measurement. For example a block 10" x 12" could be divided four times along each side; using marks every 2½" on the short side and every 3" on the long side; or it could be divided eight times using marks every 1¼" on the short side and 1½" on the long side. Draw the grid lines as above. A pattern created in this way will fill a rectangular space with a diamond grid instead of a square grid. See the SPRING BOUQUET detail on page 15.

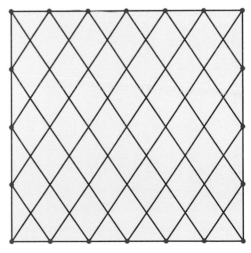

Diamond grid

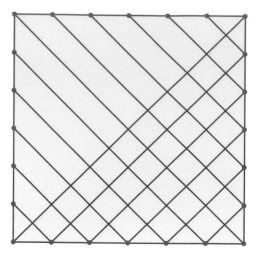

Three-quarter grid

Three-quarter Grid

A three-quarter grid is an interesting variation on the basic square grid. Use the same method as described above for dividing the sides of the block. Draw diagonal lines in one direction to fill the block. Draw diagonal lines in the other direction over half the block only. Omitting some of the lines gives a more open and asymmetrical look to the background quilting.

Hanging Diamonds

Hanging diamonds is another variation measured in the same way as the basic grid.

Use the method on page 27 for dividing the sides of the block. Draw diagonal lines, from dot to dot, in one direction, until the background is filled. Draw vertical lines, from dot to dot, to complete the pattern.

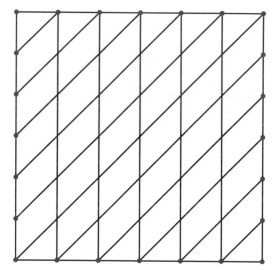

Hanging-diamond grid

Background quilting using the three-quarter grid

Spiral

Spiral background lines can be a beautiful alternative to a grid pattern. With a little adjustment to make the designs continuous, spiral patterns can be quilted by machine.

Perfect Spiral tool designed by Emily Senuta, Doreen Perkins, and the author for marking spiral background lines

1. Find the center of the block, or decide on a point to be the visual center of the design. Use a pin, coming up from the wrong side of the block, to hold the pivot point of the Perfect Spiral tool at the selected spot on the block. Place a small straight pin in the fabric to indicate the zero mark of the protractor at the edge of the tool. Draw the first line through the channel cutout.

2. Rotate the tool until you are happy with the spacing between the drawn line and the channel placement for the second line. Before drawing the second line, read the protractor to find the number of degrees the tool was rotated from the first line to the second. Make sure it is a number that will divide evenly into 360. For example, 8 or 10 degrees will be an effective spacing; 7 or 11 degrees will not come out evenly around the full block. Draw the second line.

3. Rotate the tool the same number of degrees and draw the third line. Continue to rotate the tool and mark lines an equal number of degrees apart.

4. When you reach the end of the protractor, move the little pin to the new zero mark and continue the process until the spiral design fills the space.

RIGHT: **NINE-PATCH AND SUNFLOWER, detail. Backgrounds with straight lines and spiral quilting designs.**

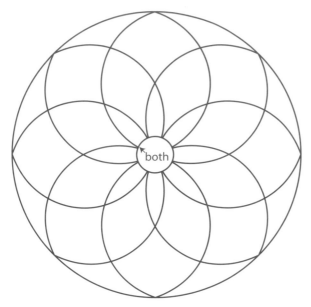

both

Perfect spiral Dahlia

Lines drawn this way can be quilted by hand, traveling between the outside spaces, or with occasional starts and stops. Machine quilters might quilt from the center out and then retrace the line, coming back in to the center, or make the design continuous by traveling in the ditch to the next line.

For pretty variations in the spiral pattern, use the straight edge of the tool for straight, radiating lines. Reverse the direction of the lines by turning the tool over and following the steps above. Or draw spirals in both directions for a dahlia effect.

Coxcomb Album block with clamshells in background

Clamshells

Clamshells are an easy pattern for free-motion machine quilting. Clamshells are also easy to quilt by hand. Place the quilt in a hoop and quilt one or two stitches at a time, turning the quilt as you go, in order to keep a smoothly curved line. Clamshells that start and stop behind an appliqué might be easier by hand.

Clamshell

Free-form

Free-form, flowing designs can be drawn to fill the background space behind an appliqué. These graceful patterns are an interesting choice to fill an irregular background space.

To begin, place the motifs where they fit or where they are needed to fill a space; then use a meandering line to connect them. Because they are connected, continuous-design free-form patterns can easily be quilted by hand, with the sewing machine, or with a longarm machine.

GINGERBREAD MEN, detail. Free-form quilted by machine.

ARIZONA SUNFLOWER, detail. Free-form quilted by hand.

Meander

A meander pattern is easy to stitch free-hand by machine. The challenge is to keep the curves smooth and the spacing even. A meander pattern can also be quilted by hand. A stencil is available to mark the pattern, if needed.

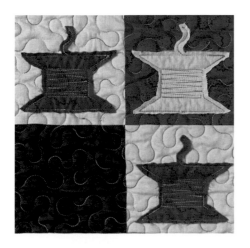

LEFT: **SPOOLS QUILT**, detail. Finished with meander quilting by machine. COLLECTION OF MARTHA CREASY

RIGHT: **POINSETTIA**, detail. Background meander pattern quilted by hand.

Quilting by the Fabric Print

Sometimes the print of a fabric can inspire the quilting design. Look for fabrics with interesting patterns and spacing to use for backgrounds, borders, and quilt linings.

DAFFODILS AND HUMMINGBIRDS. Detail, front and back. The border fabric is machine quilted following the vine pattern.

Machine Quilting for the Timid

If you are new to machine quilting, you might be surprised at how much can be done with a walking foot, turning the quilt for each change of direction, instead of quilting free-motion. Here are some tips to help you get started:

- Gather a small amount of fabric in front of the needle and let the feed dogs pull it in. Your hands should be working only to guide the fabric along its path.
- Try using the reverse button instead of turning the quilt for restitching a short line.

LEFT: Let the machine pull the fabric.

OPPOSITE LEFT AND RIGHT: VERDIGRIS. Made by Rene Jennings with patterned quilting by machine from the back.

* If your machine has a knee bar to lift the presser foot, use it to raise the foot ever so slightly after every few stitches. Repositioning the quilt will allow you to make smoother lines as you stitch along curves.

* Turn the stitch length to zero and take one extra tacking stitch at each change of direction to keep points and corners sharp.

* Use invisible thread, instead of cotton thread, when quilting in the ditch. Leaving the same cotton thread in the bobbin will give a more unified look to the back. Check to be sure the tension is balanced with each change of thread.

* To help avoid distortion when quilting long lines, quilt lines on the straight grain first, then the cross grain. Quilt bias lines last to avoid stretching.

* Turning the quilt under the machine can sometimes cause layers to shift or wrinkles to be caught in the quilting. On rare occasions, it might be worthwhile to use a small hoop to stabilize the quilt when machine quilting. Fit the quilt into the hoop with the outer ring against the machine bed and the inner ring on top of the quilt. The quilt can be turned in any direction without distorting the area being quilted.

Use a hoop to help stabilize the quilt.

Free-motion quilting can be done with a stitch-regulator foot.

The new Bernina® Stitch Regulator will help keep an even stitch length, allowing the focus of the work to be on following the pattern and creating smoothly flowing lines instead of on the stitch length. Many longarm machines have a stitch regulator and some are now computer controlled for even more accuracy of pattern.

LEFT AND OPPOSITE (QUILT ON WALL): **HONEYBEE HEAVEN, detail. Made by the author. Quilting pattern designed and digitized by Janice Bahrt. Quilted by the author on a longarm Gammill Optimum with a Statler Stitcher™.**

border designs

Continuous-line designs are always good choices for quilting on a sewing machine or a longarm. Following are some excellent design choices that you will find easy to stitch.

Straight Lines

Perhaps the very simplest way to quilt a border is with straight lines. Some wall quilts do not need an additional pattern in the border; they look complete with a solid frame. Quilting straight lines will secure the layers and control the fullness without adding another design to the mix. Begin by measuring the width of the border from the seam line to the raw edge. From this measurement, subtract the width of the binding. Divide the remaining space into three or four sections and mark quilting lines all around. These can be equally spaced or something creative, as you like. Use a walking foot to quilt each line, all the way around, with a single start and stop. Starting and stopping at a seam line will be less obvious than a start in the middle of the border. Take an extra stitch when turning the corner, to be sure it remains sharp. When the quilting is finished, tie the thread tails together and pull them to the inside of the quilt.

Ribbon

A flowing ribbon design is an easy variation on a straight line. Use a walking foot and follow the suggestions above for quilting a straight-line border. In addition, if your machine has a knee bar to lessen the pressure on the foot, use it to adjust the position of the

LEFT AND OPPOSITE: **TROPICAL BREEZES, details. Finished with straight-line quilting in the border.**

quilt as the stitching progresses. A slight change of direction after every few stitches will help keep curved lines smooth. Each line of quilting will start and stop in the same place. When the quilting is finished, tie the thread tails together and pull them to the inside.

PRECIOUS PETALS is framed with ribbon quilting in the border.

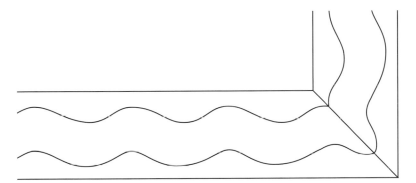

Ribbon quilting in the border

Cable

A basic cable pattern might be quilted with four, six, or eight lines stitched around the border. The cable design has more movement across the width of the border than the ribbon above, so be sure to adjust the quilt position as necessary to keep the line smooth. If the stitching begins at an intersection, where two lines cross, it is possible to continue on with a second line all around, without a stop. When the quilting is finished, tie the thread tails together and pull them to the inside.

OPPOSITE AND RIGHT: **INDIGO AND CHEDDAR STRIPPY QUILT. Notice the complex cable quilted in alternate strips.**

Star and Cable

This variation on a cable is created when the inside line takes a little jog to create a star point on the inside of the design. Stitching four lines around the quilt will complete the border. Be sure to keep the curves smooth and take an extra stitch at each star point. When the quilting is finished, tie the thread tails together and pull them to the inside.

Diamond and Cable

A diamond pattern can be added to a cable design by extending the inside curved line out to create a point and back in again. Be sure to keep the curves smooth and take an extra stitch at the outside points. Four lines around the quilt will complete the border. When the quilting is finished, tie the thread tails together and pull them to the inside.

FAR LEFT: GINGERBREAD MEN, detail. Finished with a star and cable border.

LEFT: MY HEART TO YOURS, detail. Finished with a diamond and cable border.

Swag and Tassel

A swag pattern is easy to quilt, with three or four continuous curved lines around the full border. If the stitching starts at an intersection, there should be no need to stop until the entire swag design is finished. After the swags are quilted, come back and add tassels in between and at the corners. The swag and tassel design will have more starts and stops than some of the others, but the impact is well worth it. For the cleanest look, tie the thread tails together and pull them to the inside.

Grid

Grid quilting is a good way to fill a large border, without adding another design to the quilt. It might also be a good choice to use on a busy fabric, where a fancy quilting design will not show. To begin, measure the finished border along the seam and find a number that divides evenly into that measurement, for example, two or three inches. Mark the desired spacing along each seam. Place one corner of a large square ruler against a point, positioning it so that the diagonal measurements from the border seam to the edge of the quilt are the same on each side of the ruler. Use tape to mark the base of this large triangle. Draw along two sides of the triangle, to mark the first set of lines in the border. Move the corner of the square ruler to the next mark on the border seam, line up the base of the triangle with the outside edge of the bor-

RIGHT: The swag and tassel border is a classic frame for BLOSSOMING IN A NEW CENTURY, featured on page 9.

der, and mark the next set of diagonal lines. Continue to draw a set of lines at each successive mark; eventually the lines will begin to cross each other and create a perfect grid. With machine quilting, the lines can be quilted following the same pattern, stitching in to touch the seam and out again, in a continuous line all around the quilt. Be sure that one stitch hits exactly in the border seam and then add a second stitch in the same place, before turning, to keep the corner square. Finish the grid by quilting several straight lines across each corner of the quilt.

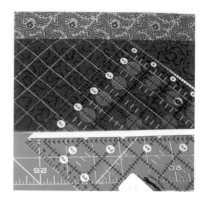

Tape on the ruler helps to keep lines "true" when marking the grid.

DEVELOPMENT OF GRID QUILTING ON BORDER

Mark a 45-degree angle, or use a mitered seam line to position the first line.

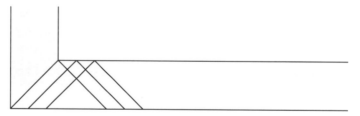

Advance the ruler a measured amount and mark again.

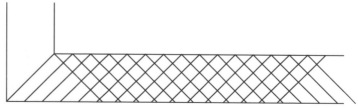

As marking progresses, a grid pattern develops.

LEFT: COXCOMB ALBUM, detail of grid quilting in the border

Picket Fence

A picket fence pattern is a combination of easy in-and-out lines, plus four straight lines, all of which can be done with a walking foot. Decide on a size that fits the scale of your quilt. Measure and mark the fence posts, and their spacing, with a ruler. Use the walking foot to quilt up one side of the post and down the other. Travel along the outside edge of the quilt to the next post and repeat all around the quilt. Add the straight lines, beginning and ending at a seam line. Take an extra stitch when turning the corner. When the quilting is finished, tie the thread tails together and pull them to the inside.

RIGHT AND BELOW: SUNFLOWER AND NINE-PATCH quilt with Picket Fence border

Vine

A vine and leaf pattern can be marked with a stencil or drawn on tear-away paper. Use free-motion quilting if you are good at it, or quilt the design, using a walking foot. Quilt one side of the stem, turn the quilt, and follow the line to stitch a leaf on that side.

Be sure to add an extra stitch at the leaf point, so that the thread does not drag across and make a blunt end. The leaf veins will be a good place to try using the reverse button on your sewing machine to retrace a line. After one side of the design is finished, repeat the process to quilt the stems and leaves on the other side. When the quilting is finished, tie the thread tails together and pull them to the inside.

WATER GARDEN is complemented by the flowing vine pattern.

Wave

A design with a dramatic change of direction will be easiest to quilt free-motion with the sewing machine or long-arm machine. Try to keep the curves smooth and take a double stitch at the points to keep them sharp. When the quilting is finished, tie the thread tails together and pull them to the inside.

LEFT AND OPPOSITE: A wave border pattern fits the mood of READY TO SAIL.

a modern mix machine & hand quilting ✤ *Anita Shackelford*

start

Wave border, designed by the author, complements the theme of READY TO SAIL.

end

special techniques

Trapunto

Trapunto can be done by hand, with the sewing machine, or on a longarm machine, and frequently more than one approach can be used in the same quilt. A padded trapunto technique can be done with any of the above methods. The basic steps are the same, regardless of how the quilt will be quilted. The only difference may be in the thread used for basting. Padded trapunto is accomplished by adding an extra layer or two of batting behind the quilt top, to raise and define specific quilting motifs.

Begin by drawing the desired quilting designs on the quilt top. Lay a piece of batting behind each area to be raised, and baste the design just inside the drawn line. If you plan to hand quilt, basting thread can be pulled out after the piece has been quilted. If the piece will be machine quilted, a washout thread will be a better choice. When every motif has been outlined, turn the top over and trim away the batting from the background areas. Each motif will be padded with a layer of batting cut to its specific shape.

Padded trapunto. Baste around the motif.

Trim close to basting stitches.

OPPOSITE AND RIGHT: HOSPITALITY, details. Made by the author.

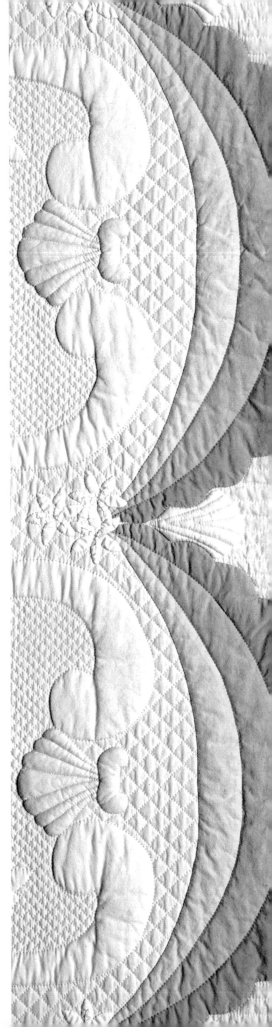

Corded trapunto can add a special effect to narrow channels such as stems and vines. Channels can be prepared by hand or with the sewing machine. Cording will require a layer of batiste behind the motif, if you choose to work by hand. Baste along both sides of the channel, stitching together the layer of batiste and the quilt top. Use a blunt needle to pull a single or double strand of yarn through the stitched channel.

Corded trapunto by hand: Use a blunt needle to pull yarn through.

Channel filled with yarn. Extra batiste is trimmed away.

Machine stitching with a double needle and washout thread makes it easy to prepare channels for corded work. Feed a small yarn or cord through the hole in the throat plate to add the cording as you sew the channel. The zigzag stitch underneath holds the cording in place until the quilt is layered and quilted. With machine basting, no batiste layer is necessary.

Thread yarn up through the throat plate for corded trapunto.

Basting with a double needle holds cording in place.

LEFT: SPRING BOUQUET, detail. Designed and appliquéd by the author.

Stuffed work is done with an interlining behind the design. The basting and quilting can be done by hand or machine; the stuffing will need to be done by hand. Baste around the motif just inside the drawn line. Use a small pair of scissors or a seam ripper to make a small hole in the batiste layer on the back and fill the basted sections with small pinches of batting. Stuffed work can be very full and round, but should be reserved for small areas such as berries and flower centers. When the work is done, trim away the extra batiste from around the design.

Preparing for quilting: After the trapunto details have been added to the quilt top, layer it with a full batting and the back, and quilt as usual. Each of the motifs should be outline quilted for greater emphasis. Choose a background-quilting pattern that will complement the mood of the quilt. Keep in mind that a finer pattern will recess the background and show off the trapunto areas to their best effect.

Stuff areas through the batiste layer.

Corner square from FEATHERED STAR shows corded and stuffed trapunto.

Stipple Quilting

Stippling is an art term that is defined as a pattern or texture created by small points or dots placed very close together. Stipple quilting can be done by hand, with a sewing machine, or with a longarm machine. The patterns can vary, but to be considered true stipple quilting, the lines of stitching should be very close together and fill the space completely.

ABOVE: PRECIOUS PETALS, detail. Hand stipple quilted by the author.

LEFT AND BELOW: SOMETHING IN RED. Made by Tammy Finkler. All patterns, including the background stipple, are quilted with a computerized longarm.

ABOVE AND RIGHT: RABBIT IN GREEN, detail. Made by Diane Gaudynski and quilted on a Bernina sewing machine.

Computer-Controlled Designs

Some of the newest sewing machines and longarm machines can stitch a digitized pattern. Computer control offers the advantage of free-motion quilting with a regulated stitch (machine makes each stitch the same length) but it is not necessary to move the quilt top as it is being quilted. The machine moves across the surface of the quilt, stitching the continuous-line design. Because the layers of the quilt are secured in a hoop or on the bars of the longarm frame, there is less risk of distortion or pleats being quilted into the top or back of the quilt. A computerized design offers straight lines, smooth curves, and uniformity of pattern in repeated motifs. It is also possible for the quilter to digitize designs for specific quilts, creating patterns that fit the mood of the fabrics and designs that are sized to fit each space.

LEFT AND ABOVE: HONEYBEE HEAVEN, detail. Made by the author. Quilting design digitized by Janice Bahrt. Quilted by the author on a longarm Gammill Optimum with a Statler Stitcher.

RIGHT: READY TO SAIL includes over 40 different designs quilted by the author on a Gammill with Statler Stitcher.

show-quality quilting

Regardless of what quilting method is used on a quilt, the criteria for good workmanship is the same.

* The design should fit and fill the space.
* The quilting design should complement the mood of the quilt.
* In traditional work, quilting stitches should be the same size, and even on the front and the back.
* If the stitch length is irregular, it should be apparent that it was a design decision.
* Starts and stops should not show. The ends should be hidden, tied off, and pulled inside.
* Straight quilting lines should be straight.
* Grid lines should be uniformly placed.
* Curved lines should be smooth.
* Ditch quilting should stay in the ditch.
* Quilting should not cause pleats, tucks, or distortion of the layers.
* In machine quilting, the tension of the top and bobbin threads should be balanced.
* Trapunto areas should be evenly filled, not overstuffed, to avoid causing distortion of background areas.
* Stipple quilting should be fine, evenly spaced, fill the area completely, and not cause distortion.
* The quilt should not be over quilted or feel stiff.
* The edges of the quilt should be straight and the corners should be square.

LEFT: BELLA, detail. Longarm quilted by Linda McCuean, 2006 $100,000 Quilting Challenge winner. PHOTO: All American Crafts (Reality Publishing, LLC.)

RIGHT: HOSPITALITY, detail. Hand quilted by the author, featuring trapunto.

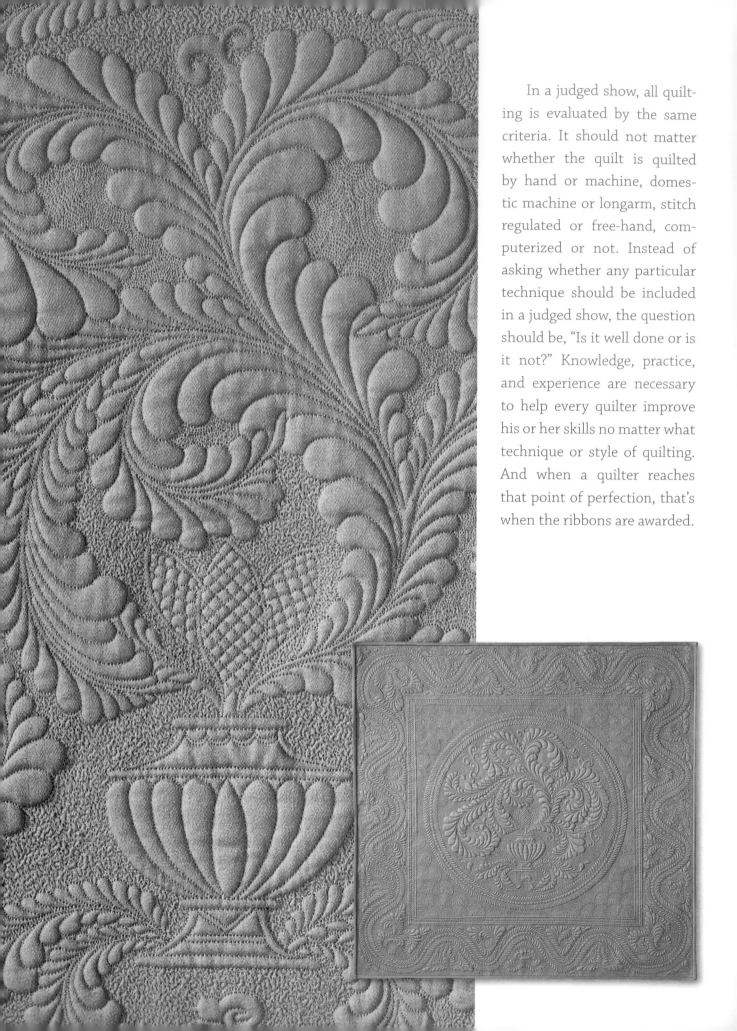

In a judged show, all quilting is evaluated by the same criteria. It should not matter whether the quilt is quilted by hand or machine, domestic machine or longarm, stitch regulated or free-hand, computerized or not. Instead of asking whether any particular technique should be included in a judged show, the question should be, "Is it well done or is it not?" Knowledge, practice, and experience are necessary to help every quilter improve his or her skills no matter what technique or style of quilting. And when a quilter reaches that point of perfection, that's when the ribbons are awarded.

ABOVE AND RIGHT: SOMETHING IN RED.
Made by Tammy Finkler, quilted on a
computerized longarm machine.

OPPOSITE LEFT: A VISIT TO PROVENCE.
Made by Diane Gaudynski, quilted on
a Bernina sewing machine.

wholecloth pillow

17" round pillow

Techniques: Stuffed trapunto, machine quilted center motif and feather wreath, hand quilted stipple background, piped edge

The round wholecloth pillow combines a machine quilted center motif and feather wreath, with hand stipple quilting in the background areas. The center motif is raised with stuffed trapunto and the seam line is accented with a matching piping.

Supplies:

Two 18" squares of muslin or plain fabric
18" square of batting
Machine quilting thread
Hand quilting thread
Between needles for hand quilting
Small hoop or frame for hand quilting
Two layers of fabric and a square of batting for quilted back, if desired
Thread for machine piecing
Small cord for piping
Pillow stuffing

LEFT: WHOLECLOTH PILLOW, center motif - Statler Stitcher design. Feather wreath designed by the author. Machine quilting by Jennifer Perdue. Hand stipple quilting by the author.

⋇ Trace the quilting motif onto the right side of the pillow top. Follow the instructions on pg. 51 for stuffed trapunto if desired. Layer the top with batting and lining and quilt the central motif and outer feather wreath, using free-motion machine quilting. Put the fabric sandwich into a quilting hoop and hand stipple the background. Assemble the layers for the pillow back and machine quilt in a random pattern or design of your choice. Draw a 17" circle around the design on the pillow front. Zigzag along the drawn line, and trim to shape.

⋇ Cut bias strips 1" wide and a total of 48" long. Fold the bias strip in half, wrong sides together; tuck the cording into the fold, and use a zipper foot to make piping for the seam.

⋇ Sew the piping around the edges of the pillow front, leaving the ends of the cording exposed. Layer the pillow front and the untrimmed pillow back, right sides together, and use the zipper foot to sew the pieces together, leaving a small opening for stuffing. Trim the excess fabric from the pillow back. Turn the pillow right side out and fill with stuffing. Pull on the cording to shorten it and pull the edges of the pillow into a softer, rounded shape. Trim the excess cording, tuck in the ends, and finish the seam by hand.

wholecloth pillow

Variations: Reverse the techniques; hand quilt the center motif and the feather wreath and use machine stippling to fill the background. Because machine quilting can overwhelm a hand-quilted line, use a contrasting thread for hand quilting and a matching or invisible thread for the background stipple.

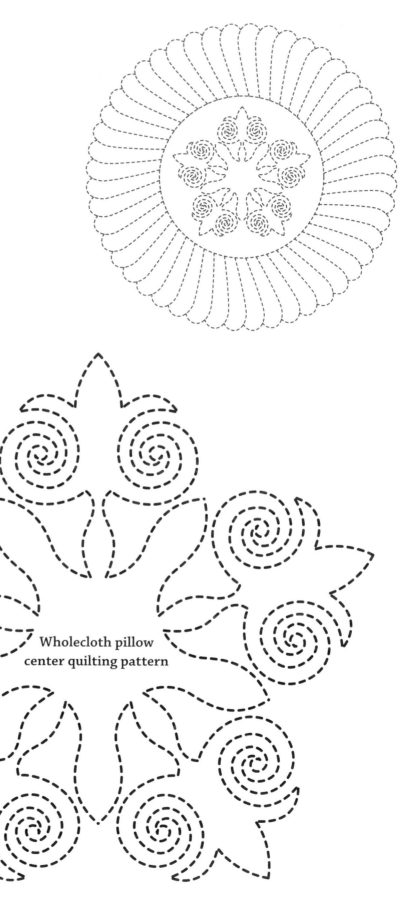

Wholecloth pillow
center quilting pattern

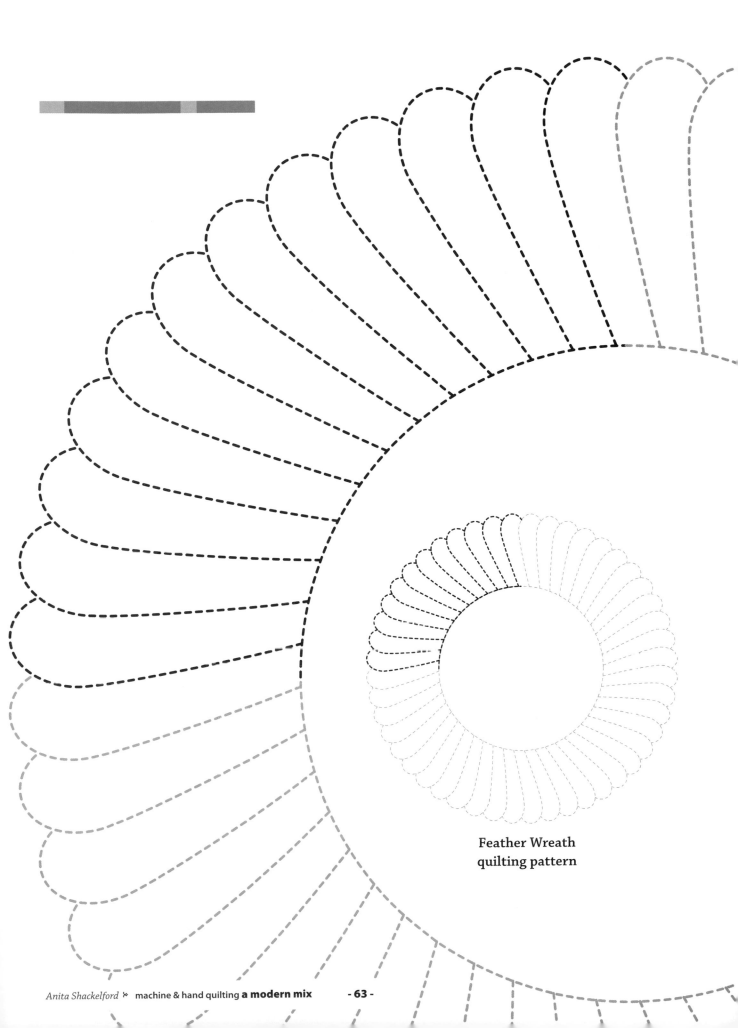

Feather Wreath
quilting pattern

hunter's square

50" x 50" quilt

Beginner Piecing, Intermediate Quilting

The simple framed square medallion is easy to piece. A beautiful toile sets the mood and the design excitement is found in the hand-quilted feathers. Machine quilting is a good choice for the straight lines through the patch-work, in the ditch, and in the cable border.

Center block 20"
Borders
> 3" toile with Four-Patch corner blocks
> 6" white with Nine-Patch corner blocks
> 6" toile outer border

Supplies:
White – 1⅜ yds.
Cut from white fabric –
> One 20½" center square
> One strip 2" x 42" wide
> Three strips 2½" x 42" wide
> Four borders 3½" x 26½"

Toile – 1½ yds. (This is a directional print so borders are cut both horizontally and vertically to keep the fabric orientation consistent.)
Cut from toile fabric –
> One strip 2" x 42" wide
> Three strips 2½" x 42" wide
> Two horizontal borders – 3½" x 20½"
> Two vertical borders – 3½" x 20½"
> Two horizontal borders – 6½" x 38½"
> Two vertical borders – 6½" x 50½"

Thread for machine piecing and finishing the binding
Machine quilting thread
Hand quilting thread
Batting 54" x 54"

PIECING THE FOUR-PATCH BLOCKS:

❈ From the white 2" strip, cut eight 2" squares.
❈ From the toile 2" strip, cut eight 2" squares.

Make sure the toile print is oriented correctly and piece 4 Four-Patch blocks.

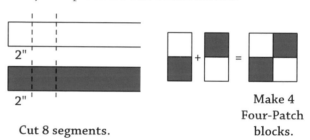

Cut 8 segments.

Make 4 Four-Patch blocks.

PIECING THE NINE-PATCH BLOCKS:

❈ From the white 2½" strip, cut sixteen 2½" squares.
❈ From the toile 2½" strip, cut twenty 2½" squares.

Make sure the toile print is oriented correctly and piece 4 Nine-Patch blocks.

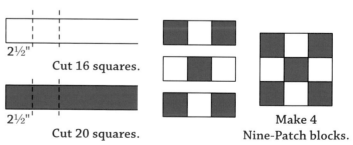

Cut 16 squares.

Cut 20 squares.

Make 4 Nine-Patch blocks.

RIGHT: **HUNTER'S SQUARE. Designed and made by the author.** Photo taken at Gaylord Opryland® Resort, Nashville, TN.

a modern mix machine & hand quilting ❈ *Anita Shackelford*

❧ Add toile borders to the top and bottom of the center square. Sew a Four-Patch block to the top and bottom of each side border, checking to see that the toile pattern is oriented correctly. Sew the borders to the center, matching the corner seams.

❧ Add white borders to the top and bottom of the quilt top. Sew a Nine-Patch block to the top and bottom of each side border and then sew the borders to the quilt. Add outer toile borders to the top and bottom of the quilt top. Sew final borders to each side.

❧ Trace the double feather wreath into the center block and a fleur de lis into each corner. Add background lines ¼" apart, radiating into each corner. Trace the pyramid patterns and small feather wreaths into each white border. Use your favorite method to transfer the cable design onto the outer border for machine quilting.

❧ Layer and baste the quilt sandwich.

❧ Using the sewing machine and walking foot, machine quilt in the ditch in all the border seams and in the small seams which divide the patchwork blocks. Machine quilt diagonal lines through the small patchwork squares. Quilt all of the feather and pyramid designs by hand. Machine quilt the outer border cable, using the walking foot and adjusting the position of the quilt as you move along, or quilt the cable free-motion. When the quilting is finished, trim the edges to straighten and to remove excess batting.

❧ Make 6 yards of bias binding 1¼" wide. Machine stitch the single-layer binding to the front of the quilt with ¼" seam. Miter the corners. Turn the binding to the back, fold the raw edge under to cover the machine stitches, and finish by hand.

hunter's square

Hunter's Square inner border quilting pattern

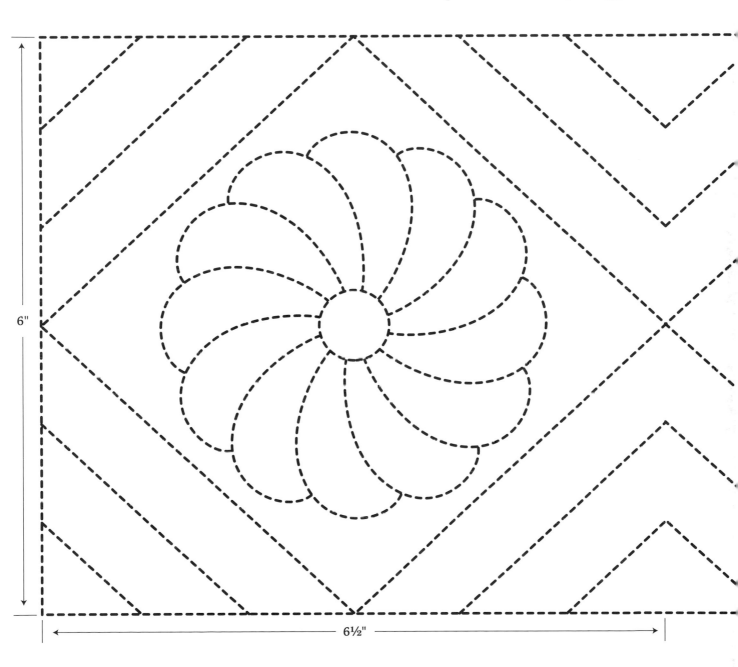

6"

6½"

OPPOSITE LEFT: HUNTER'S SQUARE. Designed and made by the author.

hunter's square

Hunter's Square
feather wreath
quilting pattern

a modern mix machine & hand quilting *Anita Shackelford*

hunter's square

a modern mix machine & hand quilting ⁂ *Anita Shackelford*

Hunter's Square
feather wreath
quilting pattern

Hunter's Square
feather wreath
quilting pattern

a modern mix machine & hand quilting ❧ *Anita Shackelford*

hunter's square

hunter's square

Hunter's Square
feather wreath
quilting pattern

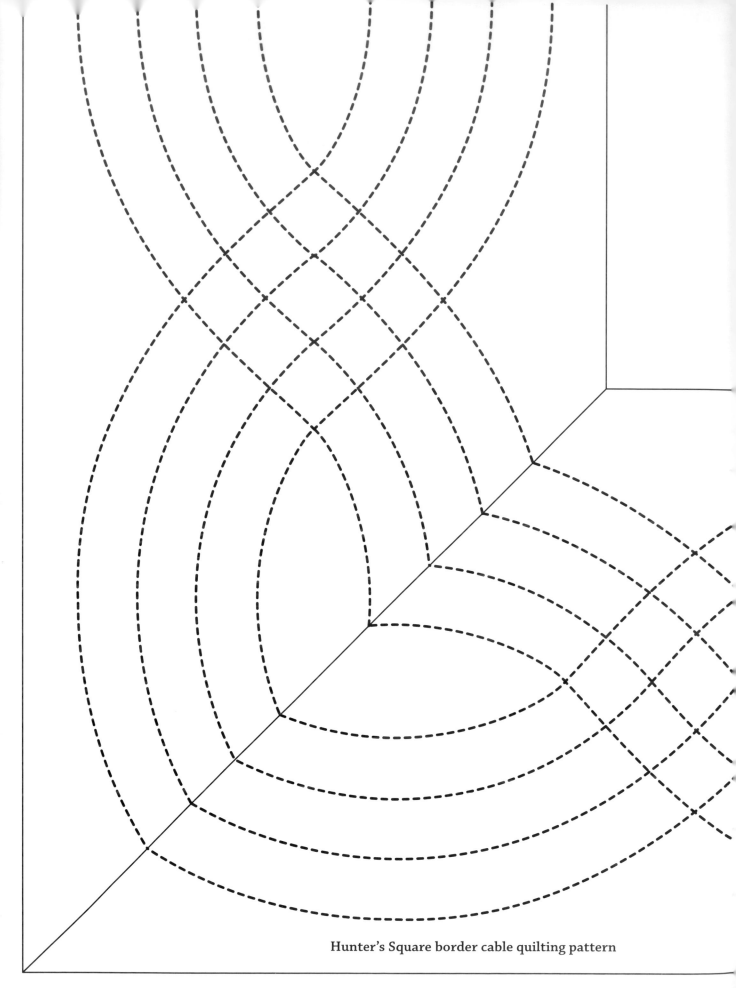

Hunter's Square border cable quilting pattern

a modern mix machine & hand quilting ⚹ *Anita Shackelford*

hunter's square

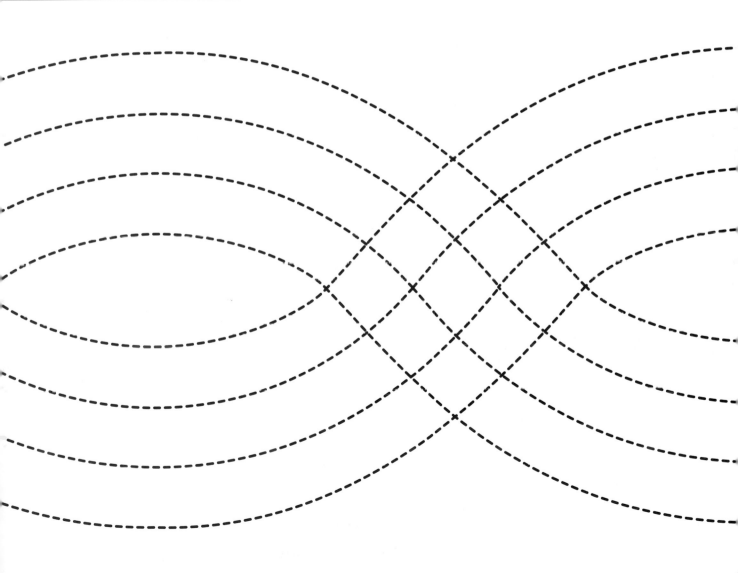

Hunter's Square
Fleur de lis quilting pattern

christmas star table runner

16" x 40" runner

Intermediate Piecing and Trapunto

The table runner combines two somewhat challenging pieced blocks with a wholecloth, trapunto block. The star blocks are quilted in the ditch by machine; additional detail is added to the patchwork pieces by hand. Hand quilting was used in the center block, where it shows to its best effect.

Supplies:

Red print – ½ yd.
Gold print – ¼ yd.
Green print – 1¼ yd.
Gold solid – 14" sq.
Invisible thread for machine quilting
Cotton thread for machine quilting
Thread for hand quilting
Thread for finishing binding
Batting for quilt – 18" x 44"
  and for trapunto, if desired – 12" square

❋ Make templates for the star blocks and piece two blocks, by hand or machine.

❋ Cut one plain block 12½" square and trace the holly quilting design into the center.

❋ If desired, follow the instructions on pg. 49 to add padded trapunto to the holly motif.

LEFT: **CHRISTMAS TABLE RUNNER. Designed and made by the author.**

❋ Use the stuffed work technique to fill the berries.

❋ Sew the three blocks together in the order shown.

❋ Cut two borders 2½" x 12½" and add to the ends of the table runner.

❋ Cut two borders 2½" x 40½" and add to long sides.

❋ Layer the top and back with a thin batting and baste to hold the layers together.

❋ Thread the machine with invisible thread on top and fill the bobbin with a cotton thread in a color to match the back. Quilt in the ditch around the stars, in the seams between blocks and in the border seams. Tie the thread ends together, thread the tails into a large needle and pull them between the layers.

❋ Quilt the star pieces by hand, as shown in the pattern. Hand quilt the holly and berry motif in the plain block and quilt ¼" inside the seam lines to frame the block.

❋ Make 3¼ yards bias binding 1¼" wide. Apply single-layer binding to the front of the quilt with ¼" seam. Miter the corners. Turn the binding to the back, fold the raw edge under to cover the machine stitches, and finish by hand.

❋ Use the machine and walking foot to quilt ¼" inside the binding to finish and frame the piece, if desired.

christmas Star table runner

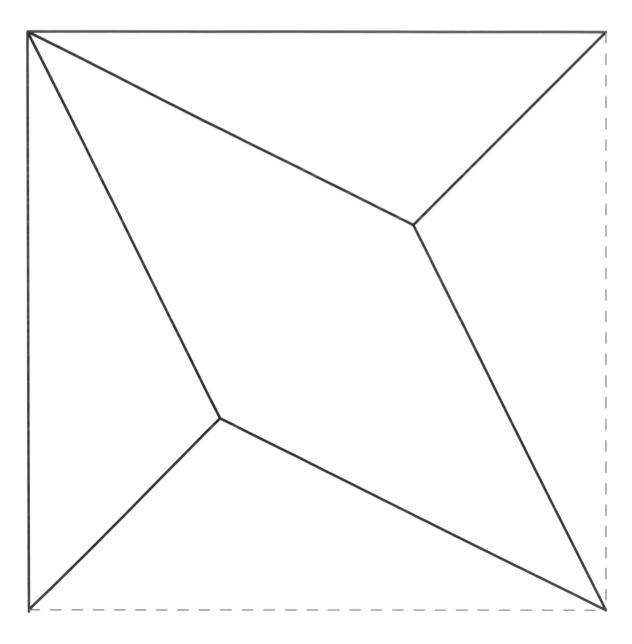

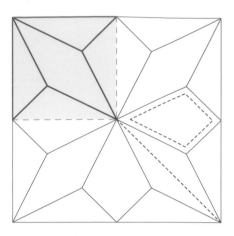

Christmas Star
table runner block pattern

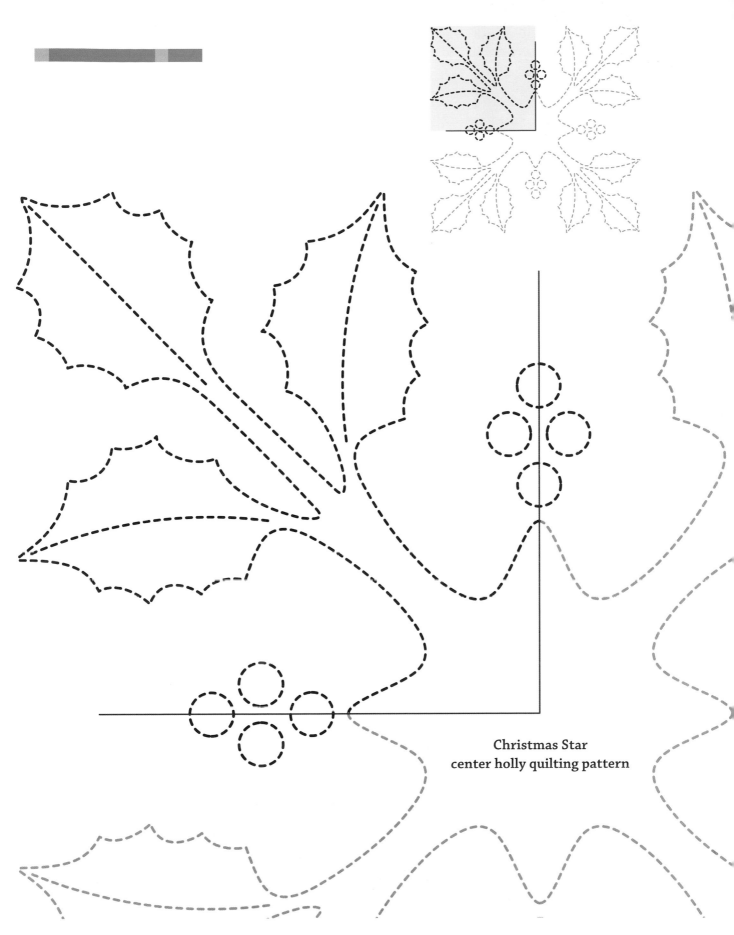

Christmas Star
center holly quilting pattern

gingerbread men

19" x 29" quilt

Easy Appliqué

A quick project, this holiday wall quilt uses a variety of hand and machine stitching and some cute embellishments. The gingerbread men are fused into place and then appliquéd with a blanket stitch, by hand or machine. Frosting lines are embroidered. The background is quilted with a free-form design and a Star and Cable pattern fills the border.

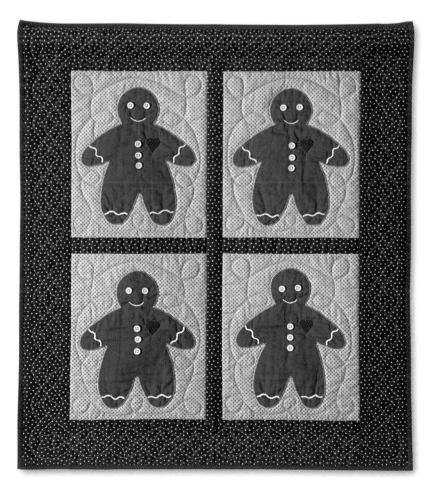

a modern mix machine & hand quilting ✂ *Anita Shackelford*

Supplies:

Tan print for background – ⅓ yd.

Brown solid for gingerbread men – ¼ yd.

Brown print for sashes and borders – 1 yd.

Red and black check for hearts and binding – ¼ yd.

Lining and sleeve – 1 yd.

Batting – 22" x 32"

20 white or ivory shirt buttons

Candlewick yarn for embroidery

Off-white thread or floss for appliqué

Thread for piecing, machine quilting, and binding

Sharps or milliner's needle for hand sewing

Large embroidery needle

❉ Cut four background blocks 9½" x 11½"

❉ Cut two sashing strips 1½" x 9½"

❉ Cut one sashing strip 1½" x 23½"

❉ Cut top and bottom borders 3½" x 19½"

❉ Cut two side borders 3½" x 29½"

❉ Trace four gingerbread men onto the paper side of fusible appliqué web. Cut out the center of the gingerbread man shape ¼" INSIDE the drawn line. Removing the fusible web from the center of the appliqué will make it softer to the touch. Press the fusible web, following the manufacturer's instructions, to the wrong side of the appliqué fabric. Cut out the gingerbread men on the drawn line.

❉ Fold the background blocks into quarters to find the center. Remove the paper from the back of the appliqué shapes. Center one gingerbread man in each block and fuse into place. Use

opposite: **Gingerbread Men. Designed and made by the author.**

a hand or machine blanket stitch to secure the edges of the appliqué. Appliqué the small hearts in place in the same manner. Use a cross-stitch to sew on the buttons. Stitch the frosting lines with candlewick yarn and a small chain stitch.

chainstitch right-handed **chainstitch left-handed**

❉ Layer and baste for quilting. If you are confident in your ditch quilting, thread the machine with a cotton thread in the top and the bobbin, and quilt the block, sashing, and border seams with the walking foot. If you are new to machine quilting, use an invisible thread on top and cotton thread in the bobbin. Quilt around the little heart and along the frosting lines by hand. The quilting around the appliqué and the free-form background lines can be done by hand or machine.

❉ The Star and Cable quilting design is a cute variation on a plain cable and fits the mood of the border fabric in this piece. It is also a good, continuous-line design for machine quilting with a walking foot.

❉ Make 3½ yards of bias binding 1¼" wide. Apply single-layer binding to the front of the quilt with a ¼" seam. Miter the corners. Turn the binding to the back, fold the raw edge under to cover the machine stitches, and finish by hand.

gingerbread men

Gingerbread Man pattern

a modern mix machine & hand quilting ⊰ *Anita Shackelford*

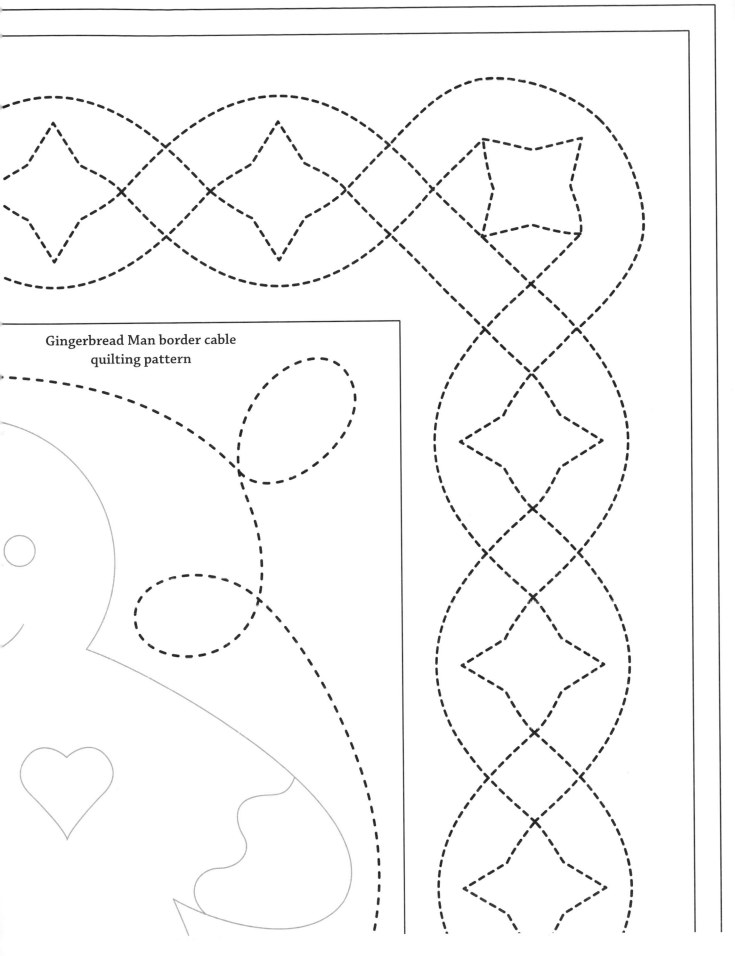

Gingerbread Man border cable
quilting pattern

feathered star

43" x 43" quilt

Advanced Piecing, Trapunto

Machine quilting is the method of choice for all the in-the-ditch quilting in the Feathered Star wall quilt. This includes seam lines within the sunflower, details in the red square and green triangles, in-the-ditch quilting around the sawtooth points, framing lines in the green border, and grid quilting in the outer border. Hand quilting fills the sunflower center, the corner blocks, and all the background details. The Narcissus quilting design includes corded and padded trapunto. A slightly darker thread color helps emphasize the floral motif.

Supplies:

Red for center, feather triangles, and binding
  – 1½ yds.

Green for center sunflower, feathered star
  points, and inner border – 1⅞ yds.

Gold for background – 1¼ yds.

Print for outer border – 1¼ yds.

Thread for machine and hand piecing and finishing the binding

Threads for hand and machine quilting

Batting for quilt – 46" x 46"
  for trapunto, if desired – 18" x 30"

Yarn – 25 yds. for cording

LEFT: **FEATHERED STAR**, detail. Designed and made by the author.

TO HAND PIECE THE SUNFLOWER CENTER:

❧ Make piecing templates as shown on page 90, with no seam allowance added. Draw around the templates on the wrong side of each fabric. Add a seam allowance around each piece, as you cut. Pin the pieces together, matching the drawn seam lines, and use a fine running stitch to piece the ring of petals.

❧ Trace the sunflower center onto freezer paper. See page 90. Cut out the paper template and iron it to the wrong side of the fabric. Cut out the circle, adding a narrow seam allowance all around. If desired, turn the seam allowance around the paper template and glue or baste it into place. Use a blindstitch to appliqué the piece into the center of the sunflower.

❧ Cut a 12½" x 12½" red center square. Fold the square into quarters and crease to make equal divisions. Center the sunflower on the background square aligning the petals with the crease marks. Appliqué the finished sunflower into place. When the appliqué is finished, turn the block over and cut away the background fabric behind the sunflower. Press seam allowances away from the center to recess the sunflower into the block.

feathered star

❧ To piece the half-square triangles for the feather edge, cut forty-four 2½" squares from each color. Layer one red square and one gold square, right sides together. Draw a line, corner to corner, on the wrong side of the gold square. Stitch ¼" on each side of the drawn line. Cut the triangles apart on the drawn line. Open and press the seam allowance to the dark side. Measure and trim each square to 1½".

❧ Cut eight background squares 1⅞" and cut in half on the diagonal to make sixteen additional background triangles. Cut four red 1½" squares.

❧ Use the templates to make the green triangles and the red diamond points.

❧ Piece eight full star points as shown (four and four reversed) and sew two to each side of the center square.

❧ Cut four 9" squares for the background corner squares. Cut one 11¾" square and cut on the diagonal in both directions to make four background triangles. Set the background pieces into the star, making sure that the center square is set on point.

❧ Cut four "floater" borders 1½" wide and insert half-square triangle details, if desired. Floater borders should measure two 1½" x 28" and two 1½" x 30".

❧ Cut two green inner borders 2½" x 29½" and two 2½" x 33½".

❧ Cut two print outer borders 5½" x 33½" and two 5½" x 43½".

❧ Layer and quilt as suggested on page 87.

❧ Trapunto can be added in the corner squares and side triangles using the patterns on pages 92–93. See pages 49–51 for trapunto techniques.

❧ Make 5 yards of bias binding 1¼" wide. Apply single-layer binding to the front of the quilt with a ¼" seam. Miter the corners. Turn the binding to the back, folding the raw edge under to cover the machine stitches, and finish by hand.

FEATHERED STAR, 43" x 43". Designed and made by the author.

feathered Star

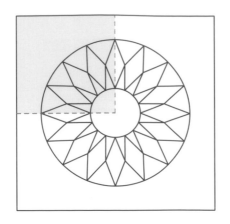

**Feathered Star
center sunflower pattern**

make templates for pieces 1, 2 & 3

✄ Fold a 3½" square of freezer paper into quarters. Open and trace ¼ of center circle into one section. Refold and cut to make template for sunflower center.

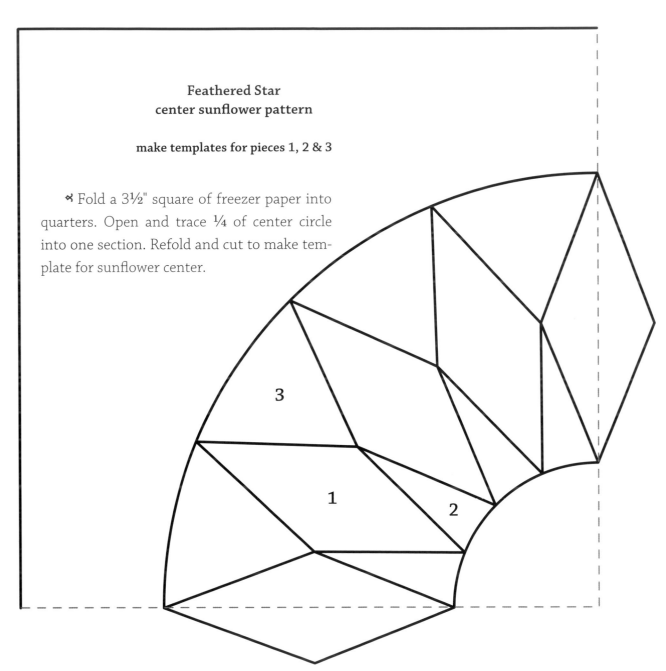

a modern mix machine & hand quilting ✄ *Anita Shackelford*

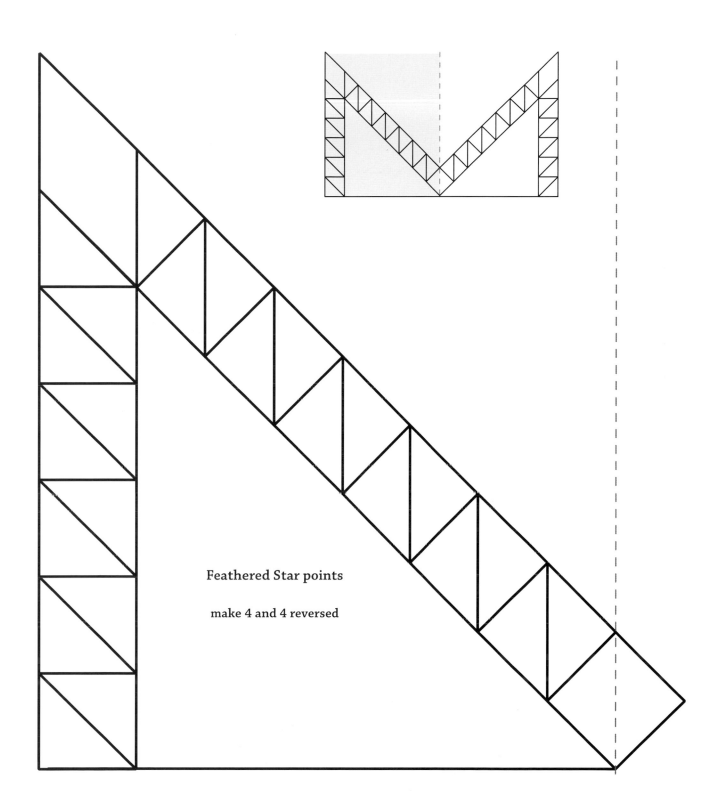

Feathered Star points

make 4 and 4 reversed

feathered Star

Feathered Star triangles
quilting pattern

Feathered Star Sunflower center
quilting pattern

Feathered Star
corner squares
quilting pattern

arizona sunflower

21" x 21" quilt

Intermediate appliqué

The sunflower wall quilt features a combination of hand and machine work in both the construction of the top and in the quilting. The needle-turn appliqué and the free-form background quilting are done by hand; the piecing and the quilting in the borders were done by machine. A Perfect Spiral quilting design and beading add beautiful detail to the flower center, while a Bernina programmed decorative stitch adds interest to the quilting in the border.

   Center block 12" square
   Sawtooth border 2"
   Outer border 2½"

Supplies:

Background block and sawtooth border –
   ½ yd.
Sunflower appliqué – 12" square
Flower center and corner blocks – ¼ yd.
Sawtooth border – scraps, ⅛ yd. total
Striped border – ½ yd.
Appliqué thread to match the sunflower
Thread for machine piecing
Quilting thread for hand and machine quilting
   Copper/brown seed beads
Batting – 24" x 24"

LEFT: ARIZONA SUNFLOWER. **Designed and made by the author. The piece was made as a sample for a retreat, hosted and taught by Lynn Kough and the author in Phoenix, Arizona.**

❧ Cut one 12½" background block.

❧ Make a template for the sunflower and trace the shape onto the right side of the appliqué fabric. Cut out the flower, with a narrow seam allowance added all around. Center the flower on the background block and appliqué into place, using the needle-turn technique.

❧ Turn the block over and cut away the background fabric behind the flower, if desired. Make a freezer-paper template for the flower center and iron it onto the wrong side of the fabric. Cut out the flower center, adding a narrow seam allowance all around. Pin the center into place on the flower and use the needle-turn technique to appliqué the center over the paper template. Cut away the fabric behind the flower center and remove the paper.

❧ Cut twelve 3" squares from background fabric and twelve from a variety of gold fabrics. To make the half-square triangle blocks, layer one gold square and one background square, right sides together. Draw a line, corner to corner, on the wrong side of the gold square. Stitch ¼" on each side of the line and cut the pieces apart on the drawn line. Open and press the seam allowance to the dark side. Measure and trim each square to 2½".

arizona Sunflower

❋ Cut four 2½" squares from dark fabric for the corner squares.

❋ Piece four sawtooth borders, in the pattern as shown. Sew the borders to the top and bottom of the quilt. Sew the dark corner squares to the top and bottom of the two side borders; sew the side borders to the quilt.

❋ Cut four borders 3" x 16½".

❋ Cut four 3" corner squares.

❋ Repeat the steps above to add the outer borders.

❋ Trace the vine quilting design into the background areas.

❋ Use a transfer paper to mark the spiral quilting design in the flower center.

❋ Layer the top, batting, and back, and baste to hold the layers together.

❋ Use a walking foot for machine quilting in the ditch in the patchwork border and in the long border seams.

❋ The serpentine border quilting lines were stitched with the #3 programmed pattern on a Bernina 1090®. Look at your machine to see what fancy stitch might work for your quilt.

❋ Quilt the free-form leaf background design and the Perfect Spiral quilting design in the flower center by hand.

❋ Stitch seed beads to the flower center, if desired.

❋ Make 2½ yards of bias binding 1¼" wide. Apply a single-layer binding to the front of the quilt with a ¼" seam. Miter the corners. Turn the binding to the back, fold the raw edge under to cover the machine stitches, and finish by hand.

Arizona Sunflower

a modern mix machine & hand quilting ❧ *Anita Shackelford*

my heart to yours

72" x 72" quilt

Beginner to Intermediate Appliqué

Choose a variety of red or pink fabrics to make this sweet sampler. The hearts are blanket stitch appliquéd and can be done by hand or machine. The diagonal line background quilting and the detail quilting within the hearts are stitched by hand. In-the-ditch quilting, long lines in the sashing, and the diamond-and-cable border are machine quilted.

    Block size 10" square
    Sashes 3" wide
    Borders 5" wide

Supplies:

White-on-white background fabric – 2 yds.
Variety of pink prints for appliqué –
    approx. 2 yds. total
Sashes, borders and binding – 3 yds.
Lining – 4¼ yds.
Fusible appliqué web, if desired
Thread or floss for blanket stitch
Hand quilting thread
Machine quilting thread
Thread for machine piecing and for hand
    finishing the binding
Batting – 80" x 80"

LEFT: **MY HEART TO YOURS. Designed and made by the author.**

❧ Cut 25 background blocks 10½" square.

❧ Trace a variety of heart designs onto the paper side of fusible appliqué web. If desired, cut out the center of the larger hearts, ¼" INSIDE the drawn line, to eliminate some of the stiffness. Press the fusible web to the wrong side of the appliqué fabric, following the manufacturer's instructions. Cut out the heart designs on the drawn lines. Use the placement suggestions of the finished quilt, or create your own designs. Fuse the hearts to the background blocks. Use a blanket stitch to appliqué the hearts by hand or machine.

❧ Cut 20 sashes 3½" x 10½".

❧ Sew together five vertical rows, using five blocks and four sashes each.

❧ Cut 4 sashes 3½" x 62½" or as long as needed.

❧ Join rows of blocks and sashes to form the center of the quilt top.

❧ Cut two borders 5½" x 62½" and add to the top and bottom.

❧ Cut two borders 5½" x 72½" and add to each side.

my heart to yours

❧ Follow the instructions on pg. 27 for marking a grid background; place marks 1¼" apart. Mark diagonal quilting lines in the background of each block. Mark the detail quilting inside the hearts.

❧ Layer the quilt top, batting, and back and baste the layers together. Machine quilt the sashing seams and border seams in the ditch. Quilt lines ⅜" inside the sashing strips.

❧ Quilt the diamond/cable design in the borders. Hand quilt the diagonal background lines and the details within the appliquéd hearts.

❧ When the quilting is finished, trim the edges to straighten and to remove excess batting.

❧ Make 8 yards of bias binding 2½" wide. Fold the binding strip in half, wrong sides together, and press to make a double-layer binding. Machine stitch the raw edge of the binding strip to the front of the quilt with a ⅜" seam. Miter the corners. Turn the binding to the back to cover the machine stitches; stitch by hand.

My Heart to Yours
diamond and cable border
quilting pattern

my heart to yours

My Heart to Yours
heart patterns

a modern mix machine & hand quilting ⊰ *Anita Shackelford*

My Heart to Yours
quilting patterns

tropical breezes

43" x 43" quilt

Intermediate Mixed Technique

Use a combination of simple piecing, folded cutwork appliqué, and bright batiks to make this tropical wall quilt. The appliqué can be stitched by hand or machine. The straight line quilting in the patchwork and in the ditch is done with the sewing machine and a walking foot. Continuous-curve quilting can be done with the walking foot or with free motion. The echo quilting around the appliqué is done by hand.

Block size: 16"
Borders 5½" wide

Supplies:

Background and other lights – total ⅝ yd.
Darks – ½ yd. total
Appliqué – ⅓ yd.
Border – 1½ yds.
10" square of freezer paper
Thread for machine piecing and
    hand appliqué
Thread for hand and machine quilting
Batting – 46" x 46"

LEFT: **TROPICAL BREEZES. The original quilt was made as a workshop sample for a retreat, hosted and taught by Sharon Stroud and the author at Lake George, New York. Designed and made by the author.**

❋ From the light fabrics, cut four 8½" squares for centers and eight 5" squares for corners.

❋ Cut four strips 2½" x 40" or 64 individual 2½" squares to make 32 Four-Patch blocks.

❋ From the dark fabrics, cut eight 5" squares for corners. Cut four strips 2½" x 40" or 64 individual 2½" squares to make 32 Four-Patch blocks. Cut two borders 6" x 32" and two borders 6" x 43".

❋ To make the Four-Patch blocks, sew one strip each of light and dark fabric together. Cut the strips into 2½" segments. Mix colors and sew pairs together, as shown, to make 32 small blocks. Be sure one light square in each Four-Patch is the background color. (See photo page 107.)

❋ To make the half-square-triangle corner blocks, layer one light square and one dark square, right sides together. Draw a line, corner to corner, on the wrong side of the light square. Stitch ¼" on each side of the drawn line. Cut the triangles apart on the drawn line. Open and press the seam allowance to the dark side. Measure and trim each square to 4½".

❋ Sew the plain center block, Four-Patch blocks, and half-square-triangle blocks together to make four large blocks, as shown.

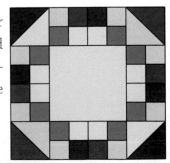

❧ Make a template for the folded cutwork appliqué by folding a 10" square of freezer paper into eighths.

❧ Open the paper and trace the pattern into one section. Refold the paper and cut the design on the drawn line.

❧ For machine appliqué, unfold the pattern and trace it onto the paper side of fusible web. There is no need to reverse the design, as folded cutwork patterns are symmetrical. Cut out the motif, position it on the background block, and fuse it into place.

❧ If you are experienced at hand appliqué, follow these instructions:

Iron the freezer-paper template to the right side of the appliqué fabric. Trace around the template to transfer the design. Before removing the paper template, lay the appliqué on top of the patchwork block. Match the folds in the paper template to the seam lines of the pieced block to find the correct position for the appliqué motif. Pin the appliqué fabric into place and then remove the paper.

Appliqué the motif, using a cut-away appliqué technique. Begin cutting around the appliqué shape, adding a narrow seam allowance. Cut only a few inches, turn the edge under, and appliqué, before cutting more. Clip the inside curves as needed. Continue until the entire shape has been appliquéd. Cut the small tear drop shapes, leaving a narrow seam allowance and reverse appliqué these areas into place.

❧ After the appliqué is complete, sew the blocks together. Add borders to the top and bottom, then to each side.

❧ Layer the top, batting, and back and baste the layers together. Machine quilt in the ditch in all of the patchwork seams; quilt diagonal lines through the square patches and add curved, continuous lines in the triangles. Quilt around the appliqué motifs and add a ¼" echo line by hand. Follow the directions on page 36 for quilting a border with straight lines to finish the quilt.

❧ Make 5 yards of bias binding 1¼" wide. Apply a single-layer binding to the front of the quilt with ¼" seam. Miter the corners. Turn the binding to the back to cover the machine stitches, and stitch by hand.

LEFT: **TROPICAL BREEZES, detail. Designed and made by the author.**

a modern mix machine & hand quilting ❧ *Anita Shackelford*

tropical breezes

long fold

Tropical Breezes
⅛ of cutwork pattern

short fold

center

tropical breezes

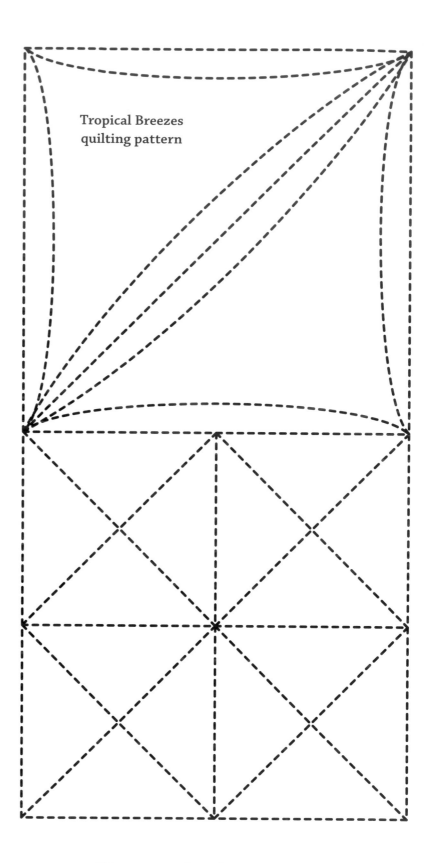

Tropical Breezes
quilting pattern

bibliography

Campbell, Elsie M. *Winning Stitches: Hand Quilting Secrets, 50 Fabulous Designs, Quilts to Make.* Layfayette, CA: C&T Publishing, Inc., 2004.

Crust, Melody and Heather Waldron Tewell. *A Fine Line: Techniques and Inspirations for Creating the Quilting Design.* Lincolnwood, IL: The Quilt Digest Press, 2001.

Gaudynski, Diane. *Guide to Machine Quilting.* Paducah, KY: American Quilter's Society, 2002.

Hargrave, Harriet. *Mastering Machine Quilting.* Lafayette, CA: C&T Publishing, Inc., 2004.

McElroy, Roxanne. *That Perfect Stitch.* Lincolnwood, IL: The Quilt Digest Press, 1998.

Morris, Patrica J. *Perfecting the Quilting Stitch : Ins & Outs.* Paducah, KY: American Quilter's Society, 1990.

Nickels, Sue. *Machine Quilting: A Primer of Techniques.* Paducah, KY: American Quilter's Society, 2003.

Parker, Mary. *Sashiko: Easy & Elegant Designs for Decorative Machine Embroidery.* Ashville, NC: Lark Books, 1999.

Shackelford, Anita. *Applique with Folded Cutwork.* Paducah, KY: American Quilter's Society, 1999.

——. *Anita Shackelford: Surface Textures.* Paducah, KY: American Quilter's Society, 1997.

——. *Coxcomb Variations.* Paducah, KY: American Quilter's Society, 2000.

——. *Infinite Feathers.* Paducah, KY: American Quilter's Society, 2002.

——. *Pennsylvania Plain & Fancy.* Bucyrus, OH: Thimble Works, 2003.

Squire, Helen. *Helen's Copy & Use Quilting Patterns.* Paducah, KY: American Quilter's Society, 2002.

Taylor, Linda. *The Ultimate Guide to Longarm Machine Quilting.* Lafayette, CA: C&T Publishing, Inc., 2002.

Thelen, Carol A. *Long-Arm Machine Quilting: The Complete Guide to Choosing, Using, and Maintaining a Long-Arm Machine.* Woodinville, WA: Martingale and Company/That Patchwork Place, 2002.

Walner, Hari. *Trapunto by Machine.* Lafayette, CA: C & T Publishing, Inc., 1996.

Wagner, Debra. *Traditional Quilts: Today's Techniques.* Iola, WI: Krause Publications, 1997.

resources

Anita Shackelford/Thimble Works

www.thimbleworks.com

   Books:

      Appliqué with Folded Cutwork

      Infinite Feathers

      Coxcomb Variations

      Pennsylvania Plain & Fancy

      Surface Textures

   Templates and Notions:

      Basic Shapes Appliqué Templates

      Infinite Feathers Quilting Design Template

      Hand Quilting Needles

      Perfect Fans & Shells

      Perfect Spiral

      Place & Trace Basket Weave Template

      Place & Trace Ribbon Weave Template

Tammy Finkler, www.tkquilting.com

   Professional longarm quilting, workshops, quilting supplies

Diane Gaudynski, www.dianegaudynski.com

   Workshops, judging, quilting books

Linda McCuean, lindamccuean@yahoo.com

   NQA certified quilt judge, master quilter, custom longarm quilting, and workshops

Andi Perejda, www.andiperejda.com

   Art quilts, patterns, workshops, judging

Emily Senuta, www.emilysenuta.com

   Perfect Fans & Shells

   Perfect Spiral

   Place & Trace Basket Weave Template

   Place & Trace Ribbon Weave Template

Sharon Stroud, www.sharonstroud.com

   Workshops, lectures, judging, quilting supplies

Linda V. Taylor, www.lequilters.com

   Longarm machines, workshops, quilting supplies

Bernina®, www.berninausa.com

   Domestic sewing machines

Gammill Quilting Systems, www.gammill.com

   Longarm quilting machines

SewBatik™, www.sewbatik.com

   Batik and hand-dyed fabrics

Statler Stitcher™, www.statlerstitcher.com

   Statler Stitcher computerized longarm quilting machines

ABOVE AND OPPOSITE: **NEW COXCOMB. Designed and appliquéd by the author. Longarm quilting by Linda V. Taylor; hand quilting by the author.**

about the author

Anita Shackelford has been a quiltmaker since 1967 and began teaching in 1980. She is an internationally recognized teacher and lecturer who loves combining applique and fine hand quilting to create new quilts in nineteenth-century style. She also enjoys using her sewing machine for many parts of the creative process and has recently added longarm quilting to the mix.

Anita has been featured on several television programs, including *American Quilter, Kaye's Quilting Friends, Linda's Electric Quilters,* and *Simply Quilts.* Her work and antique quilts from her collection have been featured in several gallery and museum exhibits.

Her quilts have been exhibited in shows across the United States, in Australia, and Japan, winning many awards, including twelve Best of Show and many for workmanship. Two of her quilts have received the Mary Krickbaum Award for best hand quilting at National Quilting Association shows. Her quilts have been published in many magazines and books.

Anita is the author of *Three Dimensional Applique and Embroidery Embellishment: Techniques For Today's Album Quilt; Anita Shackelford: Surface Textures; Applique with Folded Cutwork; Coxcomb Variations, and Infinite Feathers,* all published by American Quilter's Society.

Books and quilting tools marketed under her own business name, Thimble Works, include *Ohio Collection, Pennsylvania Plain & Fancy,* RucheMark ruching guides, Berries, Grapes & Tendrils, and the Infinite Feathers Design Template.

Anita travels extensively, teaching and lecturing for shops, guilds, and quilting conferences. She is a quilt judge, certified by NQA and qualified to judge Masterpiece quilts. She has been involved in judging shows at local, regional, and national levels, and serves as program coordinator and faculty member for NQA's Quilt Judging Seminar.

other AQS books

This is only a small selection of the books available from the American Quilter's Society. AQS books are known worldwide for timely topics, clear writing, beautiful color photos, and accurate illustrations and patterns. The following books are available from your local bookseller, quilt shop, or public library.

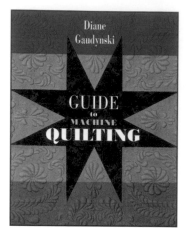

#6070   us$24.95

#7484   us$22.95

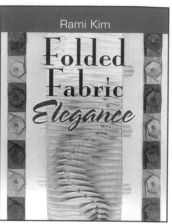

#7492   us$22.95

#7491   us$22.95

#7495   us$24.95

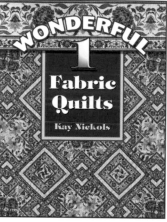

#7487   us$19.95

#7486   us$19.95

#7490   us$22.95

#6299   us$24.95

Look for these books nationally.
Call or **Visit** our Web site at

1-800-626-5420
www.AmericanQuilter.com